The Nature Kid's Guide to
HORNETS AND WASPS

DAVID ANDERSON

LP Media Inc. Publishing
Text copyright © 2026 by LP Media Inc.
All rights reserved.

For information address LP Media Inc. Publishing,
30012 Variolite St NW, Princeton MN 55371
www.lpmedia.org

Publication Data

Hornets and Wasps
The Nature Kid's Guide to Hornets and Wasps — First edition.

Summary: "Learn all about Hornets and Wasps, the Nature Kid Way"
— Provided by publisher.

ISBN: 979-8-89818-251-9

[1. Hornets and Wasps – Non-Fiction] I. Title.

Title: The Nature Kid's Guide to Hornets and Wasps

CONTENTS

WASP WONDERS

Some wasps lived at the same time as dinosaurs. They have been around a long time!

Buzz! A wasp zips right past your ear on a hot day.

Have you ever heard a wasp buzzing nearby and run the other way? Most people do. But wasps and hornets are some of the most fascinating insects on the planet, and you are about to learn just how amazing they are!

Wasps live everywhere on Earth except Antarctica. Some live alone and some live in huge groups. There are more than 30,000 kinds of wasps in the world!

All wasps have the same narrow pinched waist that makes them easy to spot. Hornets are not a different animal. They are wasps too, just the biggest members of the wasp family.

SHARP WEAPONS

A wasp can flap its wings about 200 times in just one second!

Zzzt! A wasp flicks its stinger out faster than you can blink.

A wasp's body has three main parts: a head, a middle part, and a back end. Big eyes help it see all around—even behind itself.

Strong jaws let wasps bite and chew food. Their two pairs of wings beat incredibly fast. Wasps can fly forward, backward, and even hover in place like tiny helicopters.

Only female wasps can sting. They use their stinger to catch prey and stay safe. Unlike a honey bee, a wasp can sting again and again.

PULP PIONEERS

Scritch! A wasp scrapes bits of wood off a fence with her jaws.

Some wasps build nests from paper. But they make the paper themselves! A wasp chews tiny bits of wood into a paste, then spreads it thin and lets it dry.

The dry paste turns into paper. Layer by layer, the nest grows. Some nests hang from trees. Others hide under roof edges or in attic corners.

A big nest can hold thousands of wasps. The **queen** starts the nest alone each spring, building just a few cells. Then her workers help her make it bigger all summer long.

SILENT HUNTERS

About 9 out of every 10 wasp species live all by themselves—no colony, no queen!

Whoosh! A lone wasp spots a bug and swoops down to attack.

Most wasps do not live in groups. They live and hunt all on their own. These are called **solitary** wasps.

A solitary wasp mother digs a small hole in the ground. She catches a bug and tucks it inside. Then she lays an egg right next to the bug.

When the baby hatches, it has food waiting. The mother never meets her babies, but she still gives each one a good start in life.

WORKING WASPS
FUN FACT!
Wasps eat so many crop pests, they save farmers billions of dollars every year!
12

Zoom! A wasp darts from flower to flower, covered in pollen.

Wasps help our world in big ways. Many wasps eat bugs that harm crops. Without them, there would be far too many pests munching on our food.

Wasps also visit flowers for sweet **nectar**. As they move, pollen sticks to their bodies. They carry it from plant to plant, helping flowers grow into fruits.

Some fig trees can only make seeds with the help of tiny wasps. Wasps and plants need each other to survive.

GIANT HORNETS
Asian giant hornets can fly at speeds up to 25 miles per hour—faster than you can run!
DID YOU KNOW?
14

Thud! A giant hornet slams into the side of a beehive.

The Asian giant hornet is the biggest wasp in the world. It can grow nearly 2 inches long—as long as your thumb! These hornets live in forests across Asia.

Giant hornets hunt other insects. A small group of just 30 hornets can wipe out a whole bee **colony** in hours. They use their big jaws to fight and tear.

These hornets nest underground or inside hollow trees. Workers bring food back to feed the young. The group works as a team to survive.

YELLOW JACKET

Crunch! A yellow jacket tears into a ripe apple at a picnic.

Yellow jackets are the wasps you see most at picnics. They love sweet food and meat. Their bright yellow and black stripes warn others to stay away.

These wasps build nests under the ground or inside walls and attics. By fall, a single nest can hold up to 5,000 wasps!

Yellow jackets eat many kinds of food. They catch flies, chew on fruit, and sip soda right from your cup. They are some of the boldest wasps around.

BALD-FACED BUILDERS

A bald-faced hornet nest can grow to be as big as a basketball!

Zoom! A bald-faced hornet chases a fly through the air.

Bald-faced hornets are black and white. Despite their name, they are not true hornets. They are actually wasps, and very similar to yellow jackets.

These wasps build big, round nests in trees. Each nest hangs like a gray ball made of many layers of chewed wood. Some nests hold over 400 wasps.

Bald-faced hornets guard their nest fiercely. If something gets too close, they all fly out to sting. They can even spray **venom** at an attacker's eyes!

PAPER WASPS

DID YOU KNOW?
Paper wasps can remember the faces of other wasps in their group—just like you remember your friends!

Gulp! A paper wasp sips water from the edge of a puddle.

Paper wasps get their name from the nests they make. Each nest is open at the bottom, looking like a tiny upside-down umbrella!

These wasps are long and thin with orange-brown wings. They move slowly and are not as pushy as yellow jackets. You can often watch them work from a safe distance.

Paper wasp nests stay small. One nest may have only 20 to 30 wasps. You might find one under a porch, a ledge, or even inside your mailbox.

MUD ARCHITECTS

Splat! A mud dauber presses a glob of wet mud onto a wall.

Mud daubers are solitary wasps that build with mud. They carry tiny balls of mud in their jaws, bit by bit shaping it into neat little tubes.

Inside each mud tube, the wasp puts a spider she has caught. She lays one egg on top. When the baby hatches, it eats the spider.

Mud daubers are very calm. They almost never sting people, even when you get close. You may see their mud nests on sheds, bridges, or under roofs.

TARANTULA TAKEDOWN

DID YOU KNOW?

A scientist who studies stings says the only thing to do if a tarantula hawk stings you is lie down and scream — but the pain is over in about three minutes!

Thwack! A tarantula hawk attacks a huge spider in the desert.

The tarantula hawk is a big wasp with bright orange wings. It hunts tarantulas! This fearless wasp lives in deserts and dry grasslands.

A female finds a tarantula and stings it. The sting puts the spider into a deep sleep. Then the wasp drags it to a burrow and lays an egg on its body.

The baby wasp feeds on the spider as it grows. Adult tarantula hawks are gentle around people. They mostly drink nectar from flowers. But you should be careful if you ever see one — they have one of the most painful stings of all wasps!

FUZZY VELVET

Never touch or pick up a velvet ant! Their sting is so powerful it feels like your skin is on fire!

Zip! A fuzzy, bright red bug runs across the hot sand.

Velvet ants look like fuzzy ants, but they are actually wasps! The females have no wings. Their soft, bright fur can be red, orange, or white.

These wasps live alone in dry, sandy places. A female sneaks into another insect's nest and lays her egg inside. Her baby eats the host's food to grow.

Velvet ants have a very powerful sting. Some people call them cow killers. They cannot really kill a cow, but the sting hurts so much cows act like they are dying!

JEWELED DECEIVERS

If a cuckoo wasp gets caught, it curls into a tiny armored ball that predators cannot open!

Click! A shiny wasp sneaks into a nest when no one is looking.

Cuckoo wasps are some of the prettiest insects alive. Their bodies shine like jewels, glowing in shades of green, blue, and purple.

But these wasps are sneaky. A cuckoo wasp waits for another wasp to leave its nest. Then she slips inside and lays her own egg there.

When her baby hatches, it eats the food meant for the other wasp's baby. Cuckoo wasps are named after cuckoo birds, which play the same sneaky trick on other birds.

POTTERY PROS

Each tiny pot a potter wasp builds is only about the size of a marble!

Pat, pat! A potter wasp flies to its pot with another tiny ball of mud.

Potter wasps are tiny artists. They build small pots out of mud, each one round with a narrow opening like a mini vase.

The mother fills each pot with caterpillars. She stings them to keep them still, then lays one egg inside and seals the top shut.

When the baby grows big enough, it breaks out of its little pot. Potter wasps live alone. You can find their tiny creations stuck to twigs and stems.

NIGHTTIME HUNTERS
DID YOU KNOW?
European hornets have lived in North America for over 150 years—since before the Civil War!
32

Hum! Most wasps are asleep — but a European hornet is just getting started after dark.

European hornets are one of the few wasps that fly at night. They are big and brown with yellow stripes. Bright lights pull them in after dark.

These hornets came from Europe but now live in many parts of North America. They like to nest in hollow trees or in attic walls, where it stays dark and safe.

European hornets eat beetles, grasshoppers, and other big bugs. They also chew on tree bark to drink the sweet sap inside. They are the only true hornets in North America.

STING SCALE

DID YOU KNOW?

Most wasp stings only hurt for about five to ten minutes, then the pain fades away!

Buzz! A warrior wasp lands on a branch to rest.

A scientist named Justin Schmidt let insects sting him on purpose. He wanted to rank how much each one hurt! He made a pain scale from 1 to 4.

A tiny sweat bee scores a 1. That feels like a small pinch. A paper wasp scores about a 2, and so does a yellow jacket.

The warrior wasp scores a 4—the highest! Schmidt said it feels like walking on hot coals with a nail in your foot. Luckily, most wasp stings are low on the scale.

MIMIC MASTERS

Whirr! A striped bug on a flower looks just like a wasp, but it is not.

Many animals look like wasps but are not. Hover flies have yellow and black stripes just like wasps. But they cannot sting at all!

Some moths and beetles copy wasp colors too. Bright stripes tell predators to stay away. Animals that look scary get left alone, even if they are harmless.

This trick is called mimicry. The copycats fool birds and lizards into thinking they are dangerous. It works so well that scientists have found over 100 different insects that pretend to be wasps!

WASP WISDOM

FUN
FACT!

Experts think there could be many more new wasp species waiting to be discovered in rainforests!

Crack! A wasp crawls out from a hole in an old fence post.

Wasps may seem scary, but they are truly helpful. Without them, many things in nature would fall apart. Our world needs wasps!

Many people swat or spray wasps when they see them. But most wasps will not sting unless they feel trapped. Staying calm near them is the best thing to do.

Next time you see a wasp, take a closer look. Watch how it moves and what it does. You might find that wasps are more amazing than scary after all.

GLOSSARY

solitary
Living alone, not in a group.

colony
A group of the same kind of animal living together.

queen
The female wasp that lays eggs and starts the nest.

venom
Poison that an insect pushes in with its stinger.

nectar
A sweet liquid found inside flowers.